PHYSIC GARDEN COOK BOOK

FAVOURITE MEDICINAL PLANT RECIPES

Elaine Perry

Photography by David Taylor

Dilston Physic Garden, Northumberland, UK
Registered Charity no. 1120141

Published by DPG Publications
Published in 2024
ISBN 978-1-7384368-1-1
First edition

Browse this unique handbook for enticing dishes and drinks prepared from plants growing in a garden for health and wellbeing.

Dive into a world of vibrant flavours and holistic health with our vegetarian cookbook. And enjoy sumptuous soups and salads, teas and tinctures, dips, desserts and drinks, snacks, sauces and spirits, and jams and jellies.

Recipes, lovingly composed by the curator for garden helpers, are crafted from the bountiful plants thriving in the Dilston Physic Garden.

Each easy recipe is a celebration of plant medicine and scientific evidence, Recipes showcase the remarkable benefits of the featured herbs and plants – from traditional herbalism to controlled trials and active chemicals.

And, throughout, quotations appear from writings on the plants by William Shakespeare and the famous herbalist John Gerard. So...

'Eat, Drink and Be Healthy' *and*
Harness the power of Nature's remedies

Introduction

Volunteers in our physic garden planted the idea of this booklet. They liked lunches provided in their well -deserved midday breaks and requested recipes.

Invented by the garden Curator, taking care of people as well as plants, the recipes are all accompanied by what the famous herbalist John Gerard called the 'virtues' of the plant. These are described in terms of traditional use, scientific evidence and even folklore. You could call this 'the general historie of plants' as Gerard does in his Herbal.

For each organically grown plant just one or two of the most popular recipes – all vegetarian – are included. For many recipes we don't provide precise weights and measures but use quantities appropriate to supply and demand. This intuitive approach has worked well, according to those volunteers whose approval contributed to this selection.

Many of those lunches are soups or salads often accompanied by teas and tinctures. Tinctures are alcoholic extracts, sometimes referred to here as 'spirits'. With an alcohol content in one teaspoon of less than half a unit, tinctures are often taken diluted with water.

Photos of plants in our physic garden are the best available during the writing period – the sweetcorn never ripened in time! Although most plants are familiar to everyone, illustrating them growing in a physic garden – a botanical garden devoted to the cultivation and display of medicinal plants – affirms plant health benefits beyond nutritional.

A few famous words are added to some pages of the booklet. If linked to the recipe plant there's a quote from William Shakespeare, who so often incorporated a plant in his plays and sonnets. He gleaned evidence of plant uses from John Gerard, who is also quoted. These literary and medicinal geniuses of the late 16th and early 17th centuries once lived near each other in central England. And their writings, still widely read today, hopefully enhance a booklet from a garden in Northumberland, in the north of England, created in the late 20th century.

Key books are the sources of these quotations: *A Shakespearian Botanical* by Margaret Willis (2015), *Botanical Shakespeare* by Gerit Quealy (2017) and *Gerard's Herbal* (Edited by Marcus Woodward, 1994).

Above Frontispiece of the 1636 edition of *Herball* by John Gerard **Below** Posthumous portrait of William Shakespeare by Gerard Soest, painted circa 1667.

Recipes

Above Echinacea **Below** Sunflower

Below Valerian

Recipes (in plant order)

Below Dilston Physic Garden in summer

'When roasted crabs hiss in the bowl,
   Then nightly sings the staring owl'

Loves Labour's Lost
   William Shakespeare

Apple

Malus domestica **(Rosaceae)**

Herbal medicine

Digestive, laxative, antibiotic. Bark used for tooth care.
Crab apple (*Malus sylvestris*) for gout and constipation.

Science

Clinically proven to promote weight loss and reduce blood pressure, blood glucose and cholesterol. Reduces mortality in epidemiological studies and may reduce risk of certain cancers. Chemicals include polyphenols, anti-oxidants and vitamins.

Quince (*Cydonia oblonga*) is also antibiotic as well reducing cancer risk.

Folklore

Part of religion (forbidden fruit) and fairy stories (poisoned apple), but the old saying 'an apple a day' still rings true. Crab apples associated with love and marriage.

Recipes

Quince and apple paste or JAM ▪ Equal parts of cored, de-pipped and chopped apples, including crab apples and quince, boiled in an equal volume water for two hours, adding one pound of sugar and one lemon per litre. Boil twenty minutes more and blend until fine, adding (according to taste) ground cinnamon, cloves and cardamon spices. Spoon into jam jars, seal and label.

Wassail festive cup DRINK ▪ Roast whole apples – coated in sugar and butter – in oven until soft. Add to heated cider with spices like cloves, ground cinnamon, nutmeg, cardamon, allspice and slices of lemon. Serve warm.

Right A selection of apples, and quince and apple jams

'Kidney beans are less windy
and nourish well'
John Gerard

Bean (common)
Phaseolus vulgaris (Fabaceae)

Herbal medicine
In common with other green vegetables, provides antioxidants that prevent cancer.

Science
Diuretic, hypotensive and prevents diabetes. While macuna beans treat Parkinson's disease. *Phaseolus vulgaris* also contains dopamine – the missing brain signal. Weight loss in controlled trials.

Other impact
As a leguminous plant, adds nitrogen to enrich the soil.

Recipes

Bean and potato SALAD ▪ Use leftover cooked beans and potatoes and add favourite dressing, including chopped onion and agave syrup to taste. Sprinkle with chopped chives and Russian tarragon.

Bean, pepper and tomato SOUP ▪ Fry one chopped onion and two large chopped red peppers in olive oil, add a pint of vegetable stock, a tube tomato puree and a pinch of paprika, curry powder and chilli. Boil for ten minutes and then add a few handfuls of fresh or frozen runner or broad beans. Season and sprinkle on fresh or dried basil.

Left Bean, pepper and tomato soup

CAUTION!
Raw beans can be toxic.

'The juice conveyed up the nostrils doth gently draw forth the flegme, and purgeth the head'
John Gerard

Beetroot

Beta vulgaris **(Amaranthaceae)**

Herbal medicine
For colds, constipation and cancer.

Science
Clinical evidence of increased life expectancy in prostate cancer.

Nitrate (increasing nitric oxide improving cardiac health) reduces blood pressure, heart disease and stroke.

Contains betalain chemical, an anxiolytic, anti inflammatory and anti-depressant. Also improves cognition in controlled trials.

Folklore
Aphrodisiac, root believed to be from Aphrodite, goddess of love and pleasure.

Recipes
Beet SALAD ▪ Sliced cooked beet with red peppers and tomatoes in maple syrup with chopped chilli to taste.

Borscht SOUP ▪ Fresh beets cut in pieces (including skin) and boiled in an equal amount of vegetable stock with couple of carrots and sticks of celery, adding to taste several spoons olive oil, curry powder, cardamom seeds plus date syrup to sweeten. Blend and serve hot or chilled with drizzled cream and chopped chilli.

Right Borscht soup

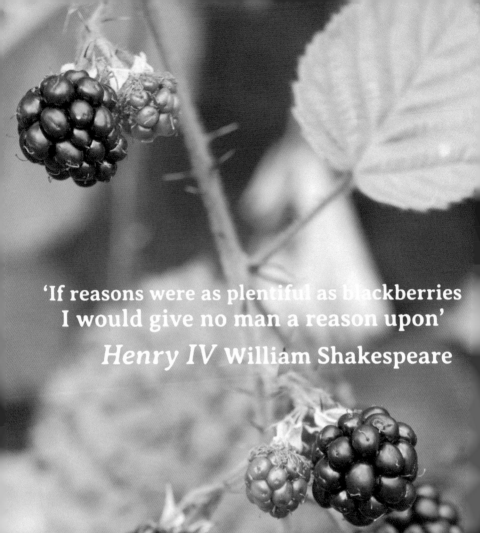

'If reasons were as plentiful as blackberries
I would give no man a reason upon'

Henry IV William Shakespeare

Blackberry

Rubus fructicosus (Rosaceae)

Herbal medicine
Protective against infections and cancer.

Science
Anthocyanin improves circulation, prevents heart disease, and retards effects of aging, particularly loss of memory.

Folklore
The devil, cast out of heaven, landed on a bramble, and cursed it. In some cultures crawling under brambles is thought to cure ailments.

Recipe
Bramble whisky SPIRIT ▪ A perfect combination of flavours, cover fresh brambles with whisky and leave for a few weeks, shaking and pressing the fruit. Pass through muslin and bottle.

Above Bramble whisky spirit

Borage

Borago officinalis (Boraginaceae)

Herbal medicine
Diuretic, useful in fevers. Soothing in lung disease. Restores adrenal glands. Increases lactation.

Science
Clinically improves symptoms of asthma. Calcium antagonist mechanism may explain traditional use in hyperactive gastrointestinal, respiratory and cardiovascular disorders. Protective effects in models of Alzheimer's.

Folklore
For courage – used by Celtic warriors. Also said to make people merry.

Recipe
Summer fruit cup DRINK ▪ Using either Pimms number 1 and lemonade or freshly squeezed fruit juices, add slices of lemon, cucumber and borage flowers.

See also **Rose** petal fragrant flower salad

Cabbage

***Brassica oleracea* (Brassicaceae)**

Herbal medicine
For rheumatic and arthritic pains. Leaves are placed on swollen joints reduce inflammation.

Science
Contains lupeol – an anti-inflammatory and anti-cancer chemical. This and other cruciferous vegetables reduce risk of certain cancers in susceptible people.

Folklore
Said to have magical properties – transporting people to spirit realms.

Recipes
Savoury coleslaw SALAD ▪ Combine grated green cabbage, carrot, cheddar cheese and shallot onion with mayonnaise for a perfect filling for baked potatoes.

Pickled red cabbage SALAD ▪ Slice thinly and simmer leaves with black currant jam vinegar, salt, caraway and coriander seeds to taste. Cool and keep in sealed jar in fridge.

Above Pickled red cabbage

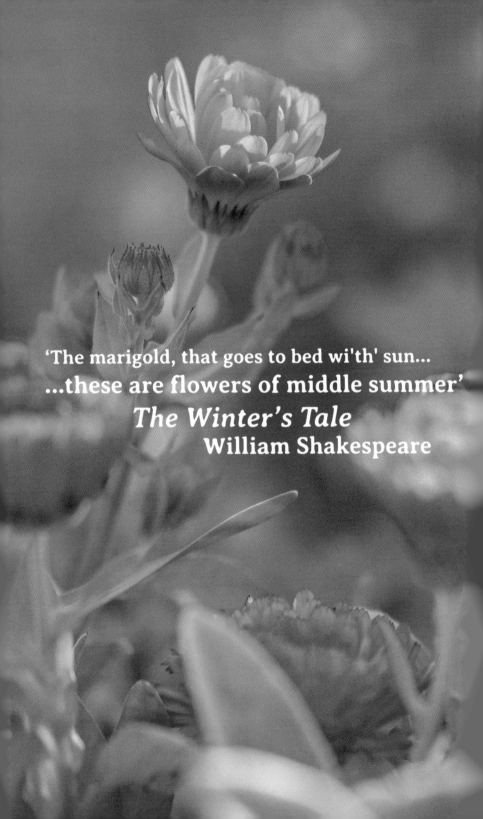

'The marigold, that goes to bed wi'th' sun...
...these are flowers of middle summer'
The Winter's Tale
William Shakespeare

Calendula/Pot marigold

Calendula officinalis **(Asteraceae)**

Herbal medicine
Antiseptic, anti-fungal, astringent and anti-inflammatory. Used externally for cuts, bruises, ulcers, skin infections, nappy rash and conjunctivitis.

Science
Clinically proven to promote wound healing and reduce radiotherapy induced dermatitis. Limited clinical evidence for treating sore nipples. Neuroprotective and counters monosodium glutamate toxicity.

Folklore
Said to facilitate prophesy and vision.

Recipe
Golden rice SALAD ▪ Basmati rice cooked with calendula flowers and turmeric, fried with curry powder, sliced onion and yellow pepper. Cool and sprinkle on sunflower seeds, golden sultanas and calendula petals.

Above Calendula petals

California poppy

Eschscholzia californica **(Papaveraceae)**

Herbal medicine
Treats sleep disorders and is analgesic as well as sedative and antispasmodic.

Science
Alkaloids include paparevine and apomorphine acting on brain signals like GABA and encephalins, control pain, but no morphine so isn't addictive.

Folklore
Flower symbolises joy, happiness, and good luck, As the state flower of California is associated with its sunny carefree lifestyle.

Recipes

Sweet flower TEA ▪ Pick a handful of orange yellow poppy petals and add near boiling water for one cup. Infuse for 5-10 min. and sweeten as required.

Sleep TEA ▪ California poppy combined with hemp, hop, lavender, lemon balm, mugwort, oat and sour cherry – one tea spoonful of fresh or dried blended herbs per cup of near boiling water.

Right Sleep tea with California poppy

'Remember William, focative is caret...
...and that's a good root'
The Merry Wives of Windsor
William Shakespeare

Carrot

Daucus carota (Apiaceae)

Herbal medicine
For vision. Antiseptic, vermifuge and treats liver disease.

Science
Eye health effects are due to vitamin A. Seed oil – anti-wrinkle, rejuvenating, immuno-stimulant and relieves PMT. Promotes heart and brain health in lab models.

Folklore
Traditional uses include colouring (e.g. cheese). The name carota means burnt as carrots were originally dark in colour, not orange as today.

Recipes
Spiced lentil and root SOUP ▪ Cook red lentils in stock and butter, curry powder and other favourite Indian spices like turmeric, ginger, coriander and garam masala. Cook a bit longer with sliced carrots and turnips.

Carrot SOUP ▪ Boil carrots in stock, blend, season, and serve with chopped coriander and swirls of cream.

Right Carrot soup

'For though the chamomile the more
it is tredden on the faster it grows,
yet youth the more it is wasted
the sooner it wears'

Henry IV part 1
William Shakespeare

Chamomile

Chamaemelum nobile (Roman)/*Chamomilla recutita* (German)
(Asteraceae)

Herbal medicine
Roman – Mild sedative, anti-convulsant (childhood) and analgesic (teething/earache). Digestive, appetite stimulant. Promotes sleep. Soothes wounds and nappy rash.

German – Induces sleep and reduces muscle spasms.

Science
Roman – Clinically verified for sleep and anxiety. Reduces blood pressure and relaxes gastrointestinal muscle in animal models. Essential oil for insomnia, anxiety and irritability.

German – Essential oil relieves fear, worry, muscular pain and skin inflammations. Clinically proven to treat generalised anxiety disorder. Clinical trial evidence for anti-depressant effects and for reducing osteoporosis pain. Chemical, Bisabololoxide, A stops cells dividing.

Folklore
Roman name acquired after discovered growing in the ruins of the coliseum in the 19th century.

Recipes

Calm TEA ▪ Dried leaf or flower of chamomile, lavender, lemon balm, motherwort, gotu kola, passionflower, skullcap and vervain. One handful per cup of near boiling water. Leave to infuse five to ten minutes.

Fresh flower TEA ▪ Pick a handful of flowers of German chamomile, infuse in 200-300ml near boiling water and sweeten if required.

Right Calm tea with chamomile

Chickpea

Cicer arietinum **(Fabaceae)**

Herbal medicine
Used for bronchitis, catarrh, cholera, constipation, diarrhoea, dyspepsia, flatulence, snakebite, sunstroke, and warts.

Science
The most effective cholesterol lowering of all leguminous vegetables. Contains novel antibiotic chemicals.

Folklore
Said to be aphrodisiac.

Recipe
Chickpea spiced SALAD ▪ Mix equal amounts of cooked chickpeas and sliced fresh vegetables like courgette, green pepper, onion, celery with dressing of olive oil, rice vinegar, agave syrup and seasoning including cumin seeds, curry powder, salt and pepper. Sprinkle on chopped parsley and Russian tarragon.

above Chickpea spiced salad

Chilli

Capsicum annuum **(Solanaceae)**

Herbal medicine
Used for digestive and arthritic conditions and other associated with pain.

Science
Works mainly by reducing substance P, a pain transmitter signal in nerves. Results from controlled trials assessing its role in treating osteoarthritis suggest that it can be effective in reducing pain and tenderness in affected joints, and has no major safety problem.

Folklore
Aztecs and Mayans held capsicum in great regard for spirituality claiming it would counter negative spells. Europeans thought is protected against vampires.

Recipes
Apple and chilli JELLY ▪ Use standard recipe for fruit jam or jelly and add dried chilli just before pouring into jars.

Chilli 'sin carne' bean SALAD ▪ Add lots of fresh chopped chilli in a favourite recipe for black beans cooked with olive oil, tomato puree, paprika, onion and garlic.

Chives

Allium schoenoprasum (Amaryllidaceae)

Herbal medicine
Medicinal value similar to other members of the onion family, particularly cardioprotective. Used for colds, flu, and appetite stimulant.

Science
Chive chemical in labs studies supports sleep and bone health and shows signs of reducing cancer. Garlic chives increase sexual activity in animal models.

Folklore
Aphrodisiac and used in fortune telling by gypsies.

Recipe
Cream cheese DIP ▪ Fresh chopped chives are the best vegetable addition to cream cheese for dips

Above Chive flower

'The fruit when it is ripe maketh the most
pleasant meats and banqueting dishes'
John Gerard

Dog or wild rose

Rosa canina (Rosaceae)

Herbal medicine
Laxative, diuretic, for coughs and antidepressant.

Science
Rich in vitamin C – ten times more than in oranges.

Clinical evidence that seeds and husks reduce pain from osteoarthritis.

Laboratory evidence of anti-inflammatory, anti-diarrheal and kidney enhancing properties.

Folklore
Rosehips used as beads in catholic priest rosaries.

Recipes
Wild rosehip SYRUP ▪
If pulping whole hips in boiling water, need to strain off the little hairs in muslin before adding an equal amount of sugar to make the syrup. Keep in fridge

Wild rosehip SPIRIT ▪
The sweetest drink is made from hips of other wild roses like the Scottish burnet rose. Cover hips with vodka, leave and shake for two to three months, strain and bottle.

Right Wild rosehip syrup

Echinacea/Coneflower

Echinacea purpura **(Asteraceae)**

Herbal medicine
Stimulates immune system. Antibacterial, antiviral, benefits skin conditions.

Science
Reduces upper respiratory infection/ colds in human studies. Alkamide chemicals act on cannabinoid receptors and are anti-inflammatory. Anxiolytic and memory enhancing effects in lab models.

Folklore
Name from the Greek 'echinos' as seed heads resemble hedgehogs. Thought to provide strength in trying times.

Recipe
Echinacea and honey SPIRIT ▪ Can use roots, leaves or flowers fresh or dried. Chop and cover in vodka, steeped and shaken for a few weeks. Strain, adding runny honey, and mix well and bottle.

Above Echinacea root

Elder

Sambuca nigra (Adoxaceae/Moschatel)

Herbal medicine
For colds, flu, hay fever, sinusitis, and fevers. anti-rheumatic.

Science
Berry clinically proven as efficient, safe and cost-effective treatment for influenza. Possible narcotic effects with advice not to sleep under the tree.

Folklore
Protective effects of the tree include keeping away evil and negative influences.

Recipes
Elderberry SPIRIT ▪ Berries boiled in water, sugar and spices like cinnamon and cloves, straining and adding an equal volume of vodka to preserve.

Elderberry JELLY ▪ Elderberries with no stalks boiled with equal amount sugar and juice lemon until set (around twenty minutes).

Above Elder flowers

'The powder of the seed
   of Fennell drunke for
certaine daies together
  fasting preserveth'
John Gerard

Fennel

Foeniculum vulgare **(Umbelliferae)**

Herbal medicine
Oestrogenic; stimulates milk production. Reduces appetite so used as a slimming aid.

Science
Clinically proven to act as a laxative, relieve irritable bowel syndrome and menstrual pain, and treat child colic.

Folklore
In Greek mythology stems used to 'steal' fire from the gods.

Recipes
Panch puran SPICE mix ▪ Combine fennel, fenugreek, nigella, cumin and black mustard seeds and stores in airtight jar. Add to soups or roast vegetables.

Fresh leaf TEA ▪ Add near boiling water to fresh fennel fronds and infuse for five to ten minutes.

Right Fennel fronds

Ginkgo

Gingko biloba (Ginkgoaceaea)

Herbal medicine
Used only in traditional Chinese medicine for asthma, coughs and digestive problems. Anti-ageing and pro-vitality.

Science
Increases blood flow to brain, improves memory. Clinically verified (many controlled trials) for improving memory in normal people, those with mild cognitive impairment and Alzheimer's disease.

Contains protective ginkgolide and bilobalide chemicals.

Not yet verified for tinnitus.

Fascinating fact
One of the oldest tree species dating back 250 million years and the only plant to survive the bomb on Hiroshima.

Recipe
Ginkgo gin with or without alcohol DRINK ▪ Fill stoppered container with fresh or dried ginkgo leaves and cover with vodka or for non alcoholic glycerine. Agitate for a few weeks, strain and bottle (both will keep indefinitely). Serve with a slice of lemon, gingko leaf, tonic and ice.

Right Gingko leaf

Hawthorn

Crataegus (Rosacaeae)

Herbal medicine
Protective against heart disease and helps digestion and sore throats.

Science
Improves cardiac function, is hypotensive and blood lipid lowering (clinically verified). Improves cognitive function. Haws rich in vitamin C and flavonoids such as quercetin.

Folklore
Inhabited by fairies according to many folklores. Associated with marriage and fertility.

Recipes
May blossom TEA ▪ Pick fresh hawthorn flowers, remove petals and add them to near boiling water. Infuse for a few minutes.

Haw Berry and crabapple JELLY ▪ Stew berries, de-stalked, with de-pipped crab apples in same volume water until soft. Strain through muslin and boil liquid with equal volume sugar until set.

Left May blossom

Lambs lettuce

Valerianella locusta **(Caprifoliaceae)**

Herbal medicine
Used as a winter or early spring tonic.

Relating to garden lettuce, lactuca sativa, sap (latex) is a sedative, soporific, calming and relieves arthritic pains and cough. Leaves for asthma, bronchitis, hyperglycaemia, and diuresis.

Science
Clinical evidence for lettuce seeds decreasing insomnia during pregnancy. Sedative and analgesic actions in lab models. Active chemical lactucarium is neurotrophic.

Folklore
Name is from resemblance of leaves to lambs' tongues. Garden lettuce was sacred in ancient Egypt, dedicated to the god Min. Considered to be aphrodisiac.

Recipe
Green SALAD ▪ Delightful addition to winter salads when garden lettuces are not yet growing.

'Hot lavender, mints,
savory, marjoram'

The Winter's Tale
William Shakespeare

Lavender

Lavandula angustfoa (Lamiaceae)

Herbal medicine
Calming, sleep-inducing, anti-depressant, anti-spasmodic. Relieves giddiness, palpitations and fatigue.

Science
Clinically verified as one of the safest essential oils, effective for anxiety, sleep (mild insomnia), cognitive function and social interaction. Anxiety effects linked to serotonin brain signal. Main active chemicals are linalool and linalyl acetate. Antiseptic and anti- inflammatory eg wound healing.

Folklore
Used in ancient Rome in baths for calming and cleansing effects. Associated with love – used by Cleopatra to seduce Anthony.

Recipes
Lavender oat biscuits SNACK ▪ Used to flavour many biscuits and cakes, a quick and easy recipe is to add dried lavender flowers and a few drops of lavender essential oil to oat biscuits in a sealed jar – keeps for up to a year.

DESSERTS ▪ Add a sprinkling of fresh or dried flowers to cream, crème brûlée or any custard pudding.

'Bawme drunk in wine...
...comforts the heart and driveth
away all melancholy and sadnesse'

John Gerard

Lemon balm

Melissa officinalis **(Lamiaceae)**

Herbal medicine
Sedative, relaxant. Reduces restlessness, excitability, headache, and palpitations.

Science
Enhances memory, analgesic, antidepressant.

Promotes sweating, digestive function and circulation.

Essential oil is calming, uplifting and clinically verified for reducing agitation. Especially safe for children.

Folklore
Used by beekeepers to keep bees calm. The name melissa means bee.

Recipes
Lemonbalmade DRINK ▪ Make strong melissa leaf tea, infused with lemon peel. Add honey or sugar to taste. When cool add lemon juice and essential oil of melissa Keeps in fridge a few days. Serve with sparkling or tonic water.

Happy TEA ▪ Lemon balm combined with lavender, rose bud, roseroot, skullcap and turmeric and prepared as for the other combination teas.

Right Happy tea with lemon balm

Peppermint

Spearmint

Mentha x piperita and spicata (Lamiaceae)

Herbal medicine

Relieves colic, nausea and vomiting. Treats nervous disorders. 'Clears' the mind.

In AROMATHERAPY the essential oil is used for mental fatigue, depression, improving concentration and reducing apathy.

Science

Clinically proven to relieve irritable bowel syndrome. Anti-spasmodic and acts on serotonin- good mood- brain signal in lab models Active oil chemicals are menthol and menthone.

Folklore

Name from Greek nymph. Romans wore mint head wreaths.

Recipes

Peppermint TEA ▪ Best made with fresh leaves, though dried herb is good too. Add near boiling water to one handful per cup and infuse for five to ten minutes. Can be served chilled.

Cucumber mint raita SALAD ▪ Grate skinned cucumber and add with fresh chopped spearmint and garlic to creamy yoghurt. Great accompaniment for curry flavoured soups or salads.

Right Peppermint flowers

'That the traveller or the wayfaring man that hath the herbe tied about him feeleth no wearisomnesse at all Many other fantasticall devices invented by Poets are to be seen in the works of the ancient writers tending to witchcraft and sorcerie.'
John Gerard on mugwort

Chinese

Common

Mugwort

(Common) Artemisia vulgaris and (Chinese) Artemisia argi
(Asteraceae)

Herbal medicine

Analgesic, sedative, hypnotic, anti-spasmodic, anti-convulsant. Treats
Parkinson's disease tremor.Promotes menstruation. Stimulates
appetite (anorexia nervosa).Anthelmintic (worm killing) and used for
moxibustion in acupuncture.

Science

Activity relating to GABA (off) and cannabinoid (good mood) brain
signals. Laboratory. studies confirm hepatoprotective, antispasmolytic,
antinociceptive(pain killing, estrogenic, cytotoxic, antibacterial, and
antifungal effects.

Folklore

In SHAMANISM, promotes clear vision and lucid dreaming. Used by the
Druids in consciousness expanding rituals.

Recipes

Mugwort and mushroom pâté SNACK ▪ Cooking with
mugwort, as the Chinese do, add fresh or dried leaves to
mushrooms fried in butter and blend. Serve on toast.

Mugwort magic SPIRIT ▪ Cover fresh leaves of Chinese
mugwort with rum. Shake daily for two weeks, strain, adding
demerara sugar, mix and bottle.

Above Mugwort magic spirit

Nasturtium/Indian Cress

Tropaeolum majus (Tropaeolaceae)

Herbal medicine
Stimulates appetite. Immuno-stimulant. Removes spots and blemishes. Urinary antiseptic. Flowers used in flower salads, seeds as a caper substitute.

Science
Anti- inflammatory. Protects against bacterial infections and liver toxicity with diuretic effects in lab models.

Folklore
Name comes from Latin for nose and twist – reaction to tasting leaves.

Recipe
Nasturtium seed caper and leek SALAD ▪ Lay out cooked leek segments and quarters of hard-boiled eggs and smother in a rich salad dressing made with added mustard, cream and sugar. Decorate with capers and parsley.

Nettle

Urtica urens **(Lamiaceae)**

Herbal medicine
Spring tonic, rich in minerals. Anti-inflammatory and analgesic.

Science
Anti-asthmatic. Reduces corpulence. Stimulates hair growth, treats eczema. Clinically proven to reduce arthritic pain and urinary tract symptoms in prostatic hyperplasia.

Folklore
Associated with female magic and healing.

Recipes

Nettle and wild garlic SOUP ▪ Fry wild garlic and new nettle leaves briefly in butter, simmer in veg stock adding a little curry powder to seasoning.Blend and serve with grated parmesan.

Spring tonic TEA ▪ New nettle shoots in spring make a surprisingly delicious, mild, spinach -flavoured tea if prepared from leaves and not stems which are woody.

'The juice of onions
snuffed up the nose,
purgeth the head and draweth
forth raw flegmaticke humors'
John Gerard

Perpetual onion

Onion

Allium (Amaryllidaceae)

Herbal medicine
Antiseptic, treatment for colds and ear infections.

Science
Cardiovascular protective: anti-hyperglycaemic and anti- lipidaemic.

Organosulfide chemicals are anti-oxidant and anti-inflammatory. Clinically proven to reduce blood pressure, lower uric acid, protect bones and promote surgical wound healing and hair growth.

Folklore
Symbol of eternal life in ancient Egypt. In magic is said to induce prophetic dreams.

Recipe
Green SALAD ▪ A vegetable which is core in so many recipes, the perpetual onion fresh leaves are fragrant and mild and enhance any spring leaf salad of lambs lettuce wild, garlic, with maybe new dandelion leaves, dressed lightly in olive oil, freshly squeezed orange, agave, salt and pepper.

'It is profitably used in a
looch or a medicine to be
licked against the old cough
and the stuffing of the lungs'
John Gerard on marjoram or oregano

'Indeed Sir,
she was the sweet marjoram
of the salad
or rather the herb of grace'

All's well that ends well
William Shakespeare

Oregano

Origanum vulgare and Origanum marjorana **(Lamiaceae)**

Herbal medicine
Digestive, reduces fever, anti-viral, relieves rheumatism and sore throats. Analgesic (toothache) and sedative (nervous disorders). Essential oil is a mental stimulant.

Science
Decreases wound infections, improves insulin response and reduces adrenaline and cortisol in controlled trials. Anti- microbial and anti-depressive as well a digestive, increases gastric acid in lab models.

Folklore
Said to increase clairvoyant dreams and to be a favourite of the goddess Aphrodite for love and happiness.

Recipes

Respiratory TEA or TINCTURE ▪ Use leaves of fresh or dried oregano, bay, ivy, peppermint, sage and thyme for tea made as other combination teas. Or make a tincture adding vodka to the herbs and strain after a few weeks.

Pasta SALAD ▪ Add chopped oregano, garlic, basil and olive oil to cooked pasta spears, with a few chopped vegetables like tomato and red pepper.

Right Respiratory tea with oregano

'Is hot and dry...
but the seeds are more
profitable for medicine...
...provoke urine

John Gerard

Parsley

Petroselenum crispum **(Umbelliferae)**

Herbal medicine
Digestive, hypotensive, sedative, for kidney disorders as well as anti-inflammatory.

Science
Applied topically reduces malasma (dark skin disfiguration) and eaten improves blood markers of urinary and anti-oxidant function in controlled trials.

Folklore
Although associated with death in Greek mythology. there was one games event where they anointed the winner with parsley.

Recipe
Parsley side SALAD ▪ Apart from adding flavour to so many dishes, an appetising salad of French flat-leaved parsley can be made with sliced onion and tomato in olive oil, salt and black pepper.

Pea

Pisum sativum **(Fabaceae/Legume)**

Herbal medicine
Used for stomach and heart health. Nutritional source of many minerals.

Science
Good source of vitamin A and C and high levels of flavone and saponin chemicals which help prevent cancer.

Folklore
In Norse mythology peas, as a gift from the god Thor were only to be eaten on Thursdays.

Recipe
Pea with mint SOUP ▪ Bring frozen petit pois to near boiling in veg. stock, blend, season and sweeten (agave) and serve with a twirl of cream and fresh mint leaves.

Above Pea with mint soup

'Notwithstanding
howsoever they be dressed
they comfort nourish
and strengthen the body'
John Gerard on potatoes

'Let the sky rain potatoes,
let it thunder to the tune of greensleeves,
hail kissing comfits'
The Merry Wives of Windsor
William Shakespeare

Potato

Solanum tuberosum **(Solanaceae)**

Herbal medicine
Used for gastrointestinal disorders and applied topically can reduce pain.

Science
Juice is analgesic -for lumbago, rheumatism, and haemorrhoids. Treats peptic ulcers.

Belongs to Solanaceae family that includes tobacco, tomato and chilli for example. Toxic if green when it contains solanine which can induce hallucinations.

Folklore
In Inca mythology Axomamma is the goddess of potato and people worshipped oddly shaped potatoes.

Recipes
Potato and leek SOUP ▪ Adding chopped rosemary, garlic and turmeric to leek and potato soup adds great flavour and colour.

Coronation new potato SALAD ▪ Dress small cooked new potatoes with chopped celery and apple in curry flavoured mayonnaise and decorate with coriander leaves.

Left Coronation new potato salad

Rhubarb

Rheum rhabarbarum (Polygonaceae)

Herbal medicine
Purgative, laxative, digestive, antispasmodic.

Science
Oestrogenic – clinically proven to reduce menopausal symptoms.
Reduces endometrial proliferation in animal models. Treatment of cancer indicated.

Folklore
In Persian mythology the parents of humanity emerged from a rhubarb plant.

Recipe
Rhubarb DESSERT ▪ As well as for crumbles and cakes, simple and delicious are red rhubarb stems stewed with fresh ginger slices, using sweet cicely instead of sugar to sweeten.

'The rose looks fair
but fairer we deem for that
sweet odeur which doth it in live'

Sonnet 54
William Shakespeare

'A rose by any other name
would smell as sweet'

Romeo and Juliet
William Shakespeare

Rose

Rosa gallica – apothecary rose (Rosaceae)

Herbal medicine
Rosehips refrigerant, relieve coughs and tickles. Essential oil is anti-depressant, aphrodisiac, nerve sedative and heart tonic.

Science
Damask rose (*Rosa damscena*) essential oil in clinical trials is anti-depressive, cognitive enhancing, relieves migraines and dysmenorrhea, as well as pain and anxiety during labour. Analgesic post-surgery. Anti bacterial activity relieves acne.

Folklore
Linked to love, beauty, purity and passion for thousands of years.

Recipes

Rose petal TEA or TINCTURE ▪ As well as a delightful tea made from aromatic rose petals (damask best) you can make an ethereal rose spirit covering petals with vodka for a few days before straining and bottling the liquid.

Rose petal fragrant flower SALAD ▪ So many edible fresh picked flower petals make a delicious and spectacular side salad – as well as rose, California poppy, evening primrose, borage, marigold, nasturtium, violet, viola or pansy for example.

For more about roses see also **dog or wild rose**

'There's rosemary for remembrance.
Pray, love, remember'

Hamlet
William Shakespeare

Rosemary

Rosemarinus officinalis (Lamiaceae)

Herbal medicine
For memory, mood and digestion. Essential oil is analgesic, disinfectant and stimulant.

Science
Clinical trial evidence indicates improves attention and memory (young and old), relieves anxiety, helps with addictive-drug withdrawal, promotes hair growth and skin health, treats gingivitis and controls blood pressure.

Lab studies indicate acts on brain nicotinic receptors for the memory signal acetylcholine. Neuroprotective, antioxidant and inhibits antibiotic resistant bacteria. Also anti-fungal.

Folklore
Associated with remembering at weddings and funerals.

Recipes
Memory TEA ▪ A combination of rosemary, blueberry, ginkgo, melissa, nigella, peppermint and turmeric is prepared as for other blended herb teas.

Rosemary oil for dressing SALADS ▪ For cooking and dressings, keep chopped rosemary leaves in coconut oil for a few weeks, strain and add to a bottle with a sprig of rosemary.

Right Memory tea with rosemary

'Not to be eaten alone in sallades
but joined with other herbs as lettuce
that it may also temper the coldnesse of them'
John Gerard on tarragon

Russian tarragon

Artemisia dracunculus **(Asteraceae)**

Herbal medicine
Stimulates appetite. Relieves toothache and is sleep inducing.

Science
Diuretic, improves glucose utilisation and prevents obesity. Sedative and improves sleep.

Folklore
With a name that means dragon, this plant was thought to repel snakes and has a root coiled like a snake.

Recipe
For SALADS ▪ With a more fiery, biting flavour than French tarragon (hence its dragon name), add fresh or dried leaves sparingly to any dish needing an uplift.

Left Russian tarragon growing at Dilston Physic Garden

'Sage is singularly good
for the head and brain,
it quickeneth the senses
and memory'
John Gerard

Sage

Salvia officinalis **(Lamiaceae)**

Herbal medicine
Used for sore throats, memory loss, menopause and diabetes

Science
Strengthens senses and memory (clinically verified). Stimulant nerve tonic, anti-depressant, hypnotic. Antiseptic – throat infections and catarrh (clinically verified for pharyngitis). Oestrogenic. Reduces salivation in Parkinson's disease.

Folklore
Great reputation for longevity. especially if taken in May.

Recipes
Memory TEA or TINCTURE ▪ Sage combined with ginkgo, mint, nigella, rosemary, turmeric and bacopa.

Sage crisps SNACK ▪ Fry fresh or dried leaves in oil or butter until crisp and sprinkle on salt and/or sugar.

Right Memory tincture with sage

Spinach

Spinacio oleracea (Chenopodiaceae)

Herbal medicine
Anti-inflammatory. Controls blood glucose. Anti-cancer.

Science
High in vitamin A and iron. Appetite suppressing in controlled trials. Anti-proliferative and anti-oxidative in lab models. Also anti-cancer, cardioprotective, anti-depressant and stress reducing in models. Active chemicals are carotenoids, zeaxanthin and lutein.

Folklore
The story that spinach has a high iron content is, surprisingly, not true.

Recipe
Spinach SOUP ▪ Simmer leaves briefly with a little stock, chopped garlic, curry powder and butter. Blend and serve with cream or grated parmesan.

Sunflower

Helianthus annuus **(Asteraceae)**

Herbal medicine
For fevers, bronchial and pulmonary disorders.

Science
Clinical trial evidence indicates high-oleic-acid sunflower seed oil has favourable outcomes on blood lipids, relevant to prevention of heart disease. Topically applied the oil prevents bacterial infections in preterm infants.

Folklore
Sunflowers were associated with Helios, the Greek god of the sun. and are now symbols of good luck.

Recipe
Sunflower seed SNACK ▪ Combine seeds with various nuts, some like salted peanuts (actually a legume not a nut) for added flavour.

Above Sunflower seed snacks

Sweet cicely

Myrhris odorata **(Apiaceae)**

Herbal medicine
Root is strongest as an antiseptic, aromatic, febrifuge, stomachic, tonic and expectorant.

Science
Anethole, a chemical occurring in this and other aniseed-flavoured plants, is a sugar substitute that can be used by diabetics.

Folklore
Aromatic scent said to be an aphrodisiac, used in 'love' medicines.

Recipe
Cicely DESSERTS ▪ Add leaves to sweeten tart fruit like rhubarb and gooseberry. Sweet cicely sorbet, made with a syrup prepared from the herb and sugar, is one of the most refreshing ice creams.

Sweetcorn

Zea mays (Poaceae)

Herbal medicine
Used for obesity, prostate problems, diuresis, as a stimulant and anti-inflammatory.

Science
Clinically there are hypoglycaemic benefits of the seed. The silk is glucose regulating in models. Oil is high in polyunsaturated fats and lowers cholesterol.

Recipe
Easy sweetcorn and bean SOUP ▪ For speed and convenience, fry onion and celery in oil and add cooked sweetcorn kernels, black beans and tomato (could all be from tins) in roughly equal proportions, with a little stock to moisten and chipotle for hot flavour.

Left Sweetcorn kernels

CAUTION!
Seeds can be infected by ergot (Claviceps purpurea), a poisonous fungus causing hallucinations, which has been used ritualistically to alter consciousness in shamanism.

'I know a bank where
the wild thyme blows,
Where oxlips and the
nodding violet grows'

A Midsummer's Night Dream
William Shakespeare

Thyme

Thymus (Lamiaceae)

Herbal medicine
Digestive, antiseptic, for coughs. Insect repellent (including mosquito). Mild sedative, for epilepsy, migraine, sciatica. Prevents nightmares.

Science
Treats bronchitis in clinical trials including in children. Anti-bacterial, anti-fungal, broncholytic and mucous-clearing in animal models.

Folklore
Used in healing rituals, to develop psychic abilities, for good luck and success. Boosts courage and confidence.

Recipe
Thyme and honey TEA ▪ Prepare using fresh leaves of lemon thyme, if you have it. and add honey. This is an excellent remedy for clearing head colds as is inhaling thyme essential oil.

Tomato

Solanum lycopersicum **(Solanaceae)**

Herbal medicine
Digestive, treats diarrhoea. Analgesic and stress relief. Detoxicant and for heart health. Aphrodisiac in Ayurveda.

Science
Clinical trial evidence for control of blood glucose and blood pressure, and for reduced risk of heart disease and cancer, particularly prostate (also ovarian, gastric and pancreatic). Enhances cognition in models. Active chemical, the carotenoid chemical lycopene is antioxidant, anti-inflammatory and antibiotic.

Folklore
Known as 'love apple', associated with Eve in the garden of Eden.

Recipe
Red, white and green SALAD ▪ Used in so many soups and salads. A favourite salad is with beet (see also Beetroot), and also fresh sliced tomato with basil and feta cheese.

The dry root is put to counterpoysons and medicines preservative **against the pestilence'**

John Gerard on valerian or setwall

Valerian

Valeriana officinalis (Caprifoliaceae)

Herbal medicine
Anti-spasmodic, hypotensive, anti-depressant, tranquillizer. Sleep inducing. Used by some as a mild psychedelic.

Science
Clinically proven for insomnia, anxiety and menopausal symptoms in controlled trials (without side effects). Increases human brain cell connectivity. Anti-convulsive and stress relieving (due to valerinic acid) in models. Acts on brain 'off' signal GABA. Increases REM (rapid eye movement sleep) associated with dreaming.

Folklore
Used in magic for protection from evil and nightmares, for purification and consecration.

Recipes
Spring leaf SALAD ▪ Valerian leaves growing before flowering are a remarkably tasty (mild and sweet) addition to lettuce salads – so unlike the malodorous root.

Valerian TINCTURE ▪ Submerge chopped cleaned root in vodka, shaking every so often for three weeks. Then sieve and bottle.

Right Valerian tincture

Walnut

Juglans (Juglandaceae)

Herbal medicine
Leaves used for skin disorders e.g. eczema, herpes, ulcers. Nuts antidepressant and sedative.

Science
Contains omega 3 fatty acids, improving blood lipids and good for heart and brain. Evidence of cognitive enhancement in human studies.

Folklore
According to the *Doctrine of Signatures* a plant carries a sign of its use, so walnut is good for brain because the nut looks like a human brain.

Recipe
Walnut pesto SAUCE ▪ As well as being added to nuts and seeds for a nibble, a delicious pesto can be made by adding crushed walnuts to chopped garlic, which can be wild garlic, grated parmesan and olive oil.

Left Walnut tree leaves

Wild garlic

Allium ursinum **(Amaryllidaceae)**

Herbal medicine
Antibiotic. Expectorant. Diuretic. Relieves arteriosclerosis.

Science
Clinically proven to reduce blood cholesterol, prevent common cold and counter lung disease. May reduce atrial fibrillation based on lab models. Neuroprotective and memory enhancing.

Folklore
Reputed protective effects against enemies and witches may be related to 'foul breath' or antibiotic effect.

Recipe
Egg parcel SNACK ▪ Apart from perking up leaf salads, sections of hard boiled eggs brushed lightly in mayonnaise and wrapped in individual wild garlic leaves make a splendid snack.

Right Wild garlic leaves

'The sugared tongue to bitter
wormwood taste
Rape of Lucretia
William Shakespeare

Wormwood

Artemisia absinthium **(Asteraceae)**

Herbal medicine
Anthelmintic (kills worms), digestive, treats gastric pain, rheumatism and fever. Analgesic and improves memory.

Science
Clinical evidence for relieving pain in osteoarthritis and promotes healing in Crohn's disease. Also anti -bacterial, anti-microbial, anti-plasmodial activity- against gastrointestinal nematodes. Neuroprotective.

Folklore
Notorious as the drink taken by French painters, absinthe is now legal in the UK. Herb worn to develop psychic powers and burned to summon spirits.

Recipe
Absinthe SPIRIT ▪ Soak wormwood and wild wormwood (mugwort) leaves in vodka for a short time for mild or longer for stronger and sweeten well as wormwood is one of the most bitter of herbs.

Appendix

Added ingredients included in some recipes (all organic):
Vegetable celery, courgette, peppers, cucumber, coriander, peanuts, and tomato
Dairy butter, cream, cream cheese, parmesan, feta, and eggs
Basics rice, olive oil, rice vinegar, salt, black pepper, agave, and maple syrup.
Spices caraway, cardamon, cinnamon, chipotle, cloves, coriander, cumin, curry powder, ginger, garam masala, paprika, and turmeric.
Stock is made from fresh fruit, veg and herbs boiled in spring water with salt for one hour, strained and kept cool for one day at most.

Disclaimer

We appreciate that readers will recognise there's no absolute need for a disclaimer in a cook book. Regarding the health benefits of the featured edible medicinal plants we intentionally omit specifying sources for the plants and other ingredients, as these choices, as for the quantities used or 'doses', are reliant on personal preferences. Likewise, avoiding potential allergies is a matter of individual discretion.

The information provided in this cookbook is intended for recipe and educational informational purposes only. While the recipes and content have been carefully curated and reviewed, the consumption of medicinal plants and herbs can have varying effects on individuals, and their safety and suitability may differ from person to person. Before incorporating any new medicinal plants or herbs into your diet, always consult with a qualified healthcare professional if you have underlying health conditions, are pregnant or nursing, or are taking medications.

It's crucial to be certain of the identity of any plant you intend to use. Misidentification can have serious health risks, as some plants may have toxic or harmful parts. Always cross-reference with authoritative plant identification sources if growing your own and, when in doubt, seek expert guidance. The quality and sources of medicinal plants and herbs can greatly impact their effectiveness and safety. Ensure that you obtain your ingredients from reputable and trusted sources.

So the authors, editors, and publishers of this cookbook are not liable for any adverse consequences, health issues, or misadventures that may arise from the use of the information and recipes contained.

Gratitude

The creation of this cookbook is a testament to the wonderful team of volunteer gardeners at Dilston Physic Garden, who embrace the joy of these dishes and beverages during their lunch breaks.

As well as capturing stunning photographs of the physic garden plants, David Taylor designed the book's layout, while Dr Nicolette Perry made invaluable contributions to the scientific sections, and Fleur Forster meticulously edited the text.

Printed in Great Britain
by Amazon

44301074R00064